CAPTURED WORLD HISTORY

THE HINDENBURG IN FLAMES

HOW A PHOTOGRAPH MARKED THE END OF THE AIRSHIP

by Michael Burgan

Content Adviser: Dan Grossman
Airship and Aviation Historian
Airships.net

COMPASS POINT BOOKS
a capstone imprint

Compass Point Books are published by Capstone,
1710 Roe Crest Drive, North Mankato, Minnesota 56003
www.mycapstone.com

Editor: Catherine Neitge
Designers: Tracy Davies McCabe and Catherine Neitge
Media Researcher: Svetlana Zhurkin
Content Adviser: Dan Grossman
Library Consultant: Kathleen Baxter
Production Specialist: Kathy McColley

Image Credits
Alamy: Aviation History Collection, 24, 56 (bottom), Diadem Images/Jonathan
Larsen, 55, Interfoto, 42; AP Photo, 12; Getty Images: Bettmann, 31, 41, General
Photographic Agency, 29, Lambert, 9, *New York Daily News* Archive, 5, 33, 39, 46, 59
(top), Sam Shere, cover, 15, 35, 58, SSPL/Planet News Archive, 45, The LIFE Picture
Collection/Pictures Inc./Arthur Cofod, 37, The LIFE Picture Collection/Sam Shere, 52;
Library of Congress, 17, 18, 19, 21, 25, 27, 51, 56 (top); Newscom: akg-images, 7,
Polaris, 53, 59 (bottom); Shutterstock: Everett Historical, 11, 22, 38, 48, 57; XNR
Productions, 13

Library of Congress Cataloging-in-Publication Data
Title: The Hindenburg in flames : how a photograph marked the end of the airship /
by Michael Burgan.
Other titles: Captured history.
Description: North Mankato, Minnesota : Compass Point Books, an imprint of
Capstone Press, [2017] | Series: Captured world history | Audience: Ages 10-15. |
Audience: Grades 4 to 6. | Includes bibliographical references and index.
Identifiers: LCCN 2016008220| ISBN 9780756554415 (library binding) |
ISBN 9780756554439 (paperback) | ISBN 9780756554453 (ebook (pdf))
Subjects: LCSH: Hindenburg (Airship)--Juvenile literature. | Aircraft accidents—New
Jersey—History—20th century—Juvenile literature. | Airships—History—Juvenile
literature. | Airships—Germany—History—Juvenile literature. | Documentary
photography—United States—History—Juvenile literature.
Classification: LCC TL659.H5 B87 2017 | DDC 363.12/492—dc23
LC record available at http://lccn.loc.gov/2016008220

Printed and bound in the USA.
009692F16

TABLE OF CONTENTS

Chapter One

A LANDING GONE WRONG

For the people of New York City, May 6, 1937, was just another Thursday, another workday in the city of 7 million people. The weather forecast for the day was mostly cloudy and cool, with showers in the morning. Readers of *The New York Times* who scanned the headlines saw news from overseas. They also saw a story about efforts in Congress to give less money to people who were out of work. The United States and most of the world were still suffering from the Great Depression. The economic downturn, which had begun in 1929, had cost millions of people their jobs.

Turning to page eight of *The Times*, readers might have noticed a small article about the delayed arrival of the airship *Hindenburg*. The giant aircraft was supposed to have docked that morning at the Naval Air Station in Lakehurst, New Jersey, about 50 miles (80 kilometers) south of New York City. But on May 5, as the *Hindenburg* neared the Atlantic coast of Canada, it ran into stiff winds that slowed its progress. As *The Times* reported, "With the dirigible slowed to 42 knots, according to reports received by American Airlines, plans to land at Lakehurst, N. J., at 6 a.m. today were abandoned." Now the airship would land at 6 p.m. that evening. The *Hindenburg*

The *Hindenburg* lazily floated over New York City on its way to the Naval Air Station in New Jersey.

was scheduled to leave that night for its return to Europe across the Atlantic Ocean. *The Times* assured readers that "speedy re-fueling … will enable the airship to start its return trip at midnight."

The *Hindenburg* had begun regularly carrying

passengers back and forth across the ocean the year before. It followed the *Graf Zeppelin*, which had earlier traveled to Lakehurst two times before beginning regular service between Germany and South America. At the time, the German airships were the only aircraft carrying passengers nonstop across the Atlantic Ocean. Passenger planes had just begun flying across the Pacific the year before, but they had to make stops along the way. And these early commercial planes could not match the size and luxury of the *Hindenburg*.

The *Hindenburg* was just over 800 feet (244 meters) long, and its hull had a diameter of 135 feet (41 m). Its four engines could propel the airship at a top speed of 84 miles (135 km) per hour—more than twice as fast as any surface ship of the era. On the inside, the *Hindenburg* and the dirigibles before it were modeled after the great steamships of the day. Since the invention of steam engines, the ocean liners had become the fastest way to cross the Atlantic Ocean. And for people who could afford to travel first class, the ships offered fine dining and beautiful public rooms.

Like an ocean liner, the *Hindenburg* had a dining room where passengers ate from china with silver knives, forks, and spoons. The food came up from the galley on the deck below and included a variety of meat, poultry, and fish. Outside the dining room,

Passengers gazed out the promenade windows from the *Hindenburg*'s lounge.

passengers could gather in several public rooms or watch the clouds pass by in one of two promenades, which were short hallways lined with windows. Art decorated the rooms, and the wallpaper in the dining room was made of silk. As on ships, the crew used naval terms. The right side of the airship was starboard, the left side was port. The ship had a helmsman, and it was commanded by a captain rather than flown by a pilot.

Unlike steamships, however, the *Hindenburg* carried fewer than 100 people, including the crew. The largest ocean liners of the day easily carried more than 1,000 passengers, with the luxurious *Queen Mary* carrying nearly 2,000. But traveling with fewer passengers came at a cost. A ticket on the *Hindenburg* to North America from Europe was $450 in 1937. In comparison, first-class passengers could travel on a German ship for as little as $157 and on the *Queen Mary* for about $240. A third-class ticket cost less than $100.

Since the airship traveled in the air, its builders had to be concerned with weight. Many items were made from duralumin, a strong, light metal alloy. The German designers of the *Hindenburg* also had to worry about the risk of fire. The airship was kept aloft by about 7 million cubic feet (198,200 cubic meters) of hydrogen. This lighter-than-air gas is highly flammable, and even the smallest spark could set the airship ablaze. To prevent fires, the crew wore shoes with rubber or felt soles when they were working so they would not produce static electricity. Before they boarded, passengers had to turn over all matches and lighters so they could be safely locked away. Despite the risks of using hydrogen, the owners and crew of the *Hindenburg* believed the airship was safe to fly.

For the people of New York, the *Hindenburg*'s 12-hour delay meant they could enjoy the sight of the

The German designers of the *Hindenburg* also had to worry about the risk of fire.

The *Hindenburg*, with its Nazi swastikas on the tail, flew over Manhattan and the Hudson River.

cigar-shaped airship gliding overhead. Even though airships were not new, their size and advanced technology stirred interest. And in the United States, they were rare. The U.S. Navy had used several for training and reconnaissance, and as airborne aircraft carriers, but no American-made dirigible had ever carried paying passengers.

A German, Count Ferdinand von Zeppelin, had built the first successful airship, and his company had perfected them for passenger travel. All the airships the company built, including the *Hindenburg*, were sometimes called zeppelins.

Around 3 p.m. on May 6, the *Hindenburg* made its way over New York City. Many people below looked up and waved, while drivers honked their horns. The *Hindenburg* flew so close to the Empire State Building that passengers looking out the promenade windows could see people on the skyscraper's outside deck. Some were raising their cameras to photograph the passing airship. Some passengers looked for familiar sights, such as the Statue of Liberty, and newcomers to New York admired the skyline and ocean liners sitting at the docks.

Just after 3:30 p.m. the airship left New York City and headed toward Lakehurst. As the *Hindenburg* crossed the Hudson River, the ships below blew their horns and whistles in welcome. Some passengers went back to their cabins to prepare for their arrival in New Jersey. A few went to the airship's specially designed smoking room. Passengers on earlier zeppelins had complained about not being allowed to smoke. So the *Hindenburg* had a room that was separated from the rest of the airship with a special entryway. A crew member opened and shut the doors and controlled the only lighter available to passengers during the flight.

A small plane escorted the *Hindenburg* to the Lakehurst landing site.

By 4:15 p.m. the *Hindenburg* was nearing Lakehurst Naval Air Station. In 1921 the Navy had made the base the headquarters for all its inflatable aircraft. Lakehurst was also the landing site for all zeppelins arriving from Germany. The airships approached a large metal tower in the airfield called a landing or mooring mast. The nose of the airships attached to the mast.

The *Hindenburg*, however, was still several hours away from docking at the mast. As it approached Lakehurst, the weather turned bad, with thunderstorms in the area. At 5:42 p.m. the commander at Lakehurst, Charles Rosendahl, sent a message to the airship: "CONDITIONS STILL

UNSETTLED RECOMMEND DELAY LANDING UNTIL FURTHER WORD FROM STATION ADVISE YOUR DECISION." Rosendahl had captained surface ships before volunteering to serve in the Navy's airship program in 1923. He commanded two of the Navy's dirigibles and had flown several times on the *Hindenburg*.

From the *Hindenburg*, Captain Max Pruss radioed back this response: "WE WILL WAIT TILL YOU REPORT THAT LANDING CONDITIONS ARE BETTER." Like Rosendahl, Pruss had years of experience on dirigibles. He had taken command of the *Hindenburg* late in 1936. While he waited for the weather to clear, Pruss had the helmsman steer the airship away from Lakehurst and toward the New Jersey shore.

At Lakehurst Naval Station, a group of people was also hoping the weather would improve so the *Hindenburg* could land. Relatives of some of the passengers eagerly waited to see their loved ones, and newspaper photographers wanted to get pictures. A Chicago radio station had sent a reporter and his engineer, and several news companies had movie cameras there to record the landing. Also waiting were more than 200 workers, sailors, and civilians, who would guide the airship to the mooring mast and down to the ground.

At 6:22 p.m. Rosendahl sent word to the *Hindenburg* that the weather had improved and the airship could

Captain Max Pruss crossed the Atlantic Ocean nearly 200 times in his career.

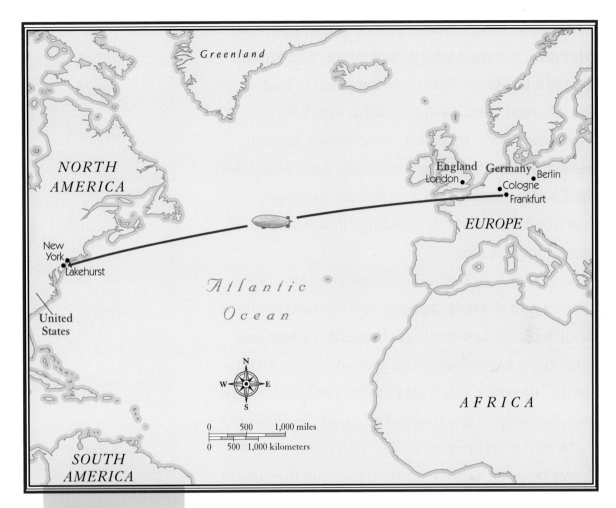

Greenland

NORTH
AMERICA

England   Germany
London   •   •Berlin
           Cologne•
           •Frankfurt

EUROPE

New
York•
 •Lakehurst

United
States

Atlantic

Ocean

N
W   E
S

AFRICA

0   500   1,000 miles
0   500   1,000 kilometers

SOUTH
AMERICA

Disaster occurred on the *Hindenburg*'s 63rd flight.

land. The airship turned and headed north toward
Lakehurst. Just after 7 p.m., Pruss received a message
from the ground urging him to land as soon as
possible, before the weather could worsen. Light rain
still fell, but the thunderstorms had left the area. The
German captain took his airship once around the
field, flying at an altitude of 600 feet (183 m). Then, as
the *Hindenburg* approached the mooring mast, Pruss
ordered his crew to reverse the engines, to slow the
airship. At 7:21 p.m. crew members began dropping
thick mooring lines to the station's landing crew.

Some passengers were standing at the promenade windows, waving to the crowd below. The airship was still in the air, but it was expected to land at any moment. To Rosendahl and others who had experience with dirigibles, its approach seemed perfect. Recording his observations for a broadcast, the Chicago radio reporter, Herbert Morrison, described the slowly descending *Hindenburg* as a "great floating palace."

But on the ground, a sailor noticed some of the covering on the hull flapping. A Navy officer on the mooring mast saw the same thing. At almost the same time, a member of the ground crew noticed a spark "like static electricity" along the bottom of the hull. Seconds later a flame shot out of the ship's top.

"It was a brilliant burst of flame resembling a flower opening rapidly into bloom," said Rosendahl. "I knew at once the ship was doomed." As the flame grew, some on the ground heard a muffled explosion. Speaking into his microphone, Morrison went from calmly describing the scene to shouting: "It burst into flames! Get out of the way! Get out of the way! … It's burning, bursting into flames … This is one of the worst catastrophes in the world. And oh, it's … burning, oh, four or five hundred feet into the sky. It's a terrific crash, ladies and gentlemen. The smoke and the flames now and the frame is crashing to the ground, not quite to the mooring mast.

"I knew at once the ship was doomed."

The *Hindenburg* exploded in a "brilliant burst of flame."

Oh, the humanity and all the passengers screaming around here."

As Morrison and others on the ground watched the scene with horror, the newspaper photographers captured the tragedy on film. One of them would take one of the most famous photos of the 20th century, showing the fiery end of the *Hindenburg*, and of commercial airships.

ChapterTwo
RISE OF THE AIRSHIP

Almost three decades before the Wright Brothers made their historic first airplane flight in 1903 at Kitty Hawk, North Carolina, Count Ferdinand von Zeppelin had a vision. The German general imagined an airship the size of an ocean liner that could carry mail and passengers over long distances. Lifting the ship into the skies would be hundreds of thousands of cubic feet of a lighter-than-air gas. From the beginning, Zeppelin imagined the gas filling a huge balloon made of separate compartments, called cells. The cells would sit inside a frame of metal girders. Cloth would cover the cells and the girders. The airship would have engines to power it and a pilot to steer it.

Zeppelin's airship was called a rigid airship because of the metal frame, which kept the craft's cigar shape. The blimp, a later kind of airship, had no metal framework around the gas compartment. Zeppelin's design was also called a dirigible, from the French word *diriger*—"to steer."

When Zeppelin came up with his idea, using balloons to fly was nothing new. In 1783 brothers Joseph-Michel and Jacques-Ètienne Montgolfier created a hot-air balloon. They used heat from a fire set beneath an opening at the bottom of the balloon.

A balloon ascended over Lyon, France, in early 1784.

Warm air filled the balloon and lifted it off the ground. Heating air makes it weigh less than the cooler air around it, and this principle took the Montgolfiers' balloon into the sky. After sending several animals up on test flights, the brothers recruited two men to become the first humans to fly. Soon after this flight, a manned balloon filled with hydrogen rose into the air. Benjamin Franklin, the

great U.S. statesman and inventor, saw the first of these passenger flights. "We observed it lift off in the most majestic manner," he wrote. "When it reached around 250 feet (76 m) in altitude, the intrepid voyagers lowered their hats to salute the spectators. We could not help feeling a certain mixture of awe and admiration."

A decade before Zeppelin envisioned his airship, he flew in a hot-air balloon while visiting the United States. The Civil War was under way, and the general met John Steiner, a German-born soldier who

Balloons were used for reconnaisance missions during the Civil War.

Count Ferdinand von Zeppelin had a long army career before developing a rigid airship.

had flown a balloon for the Union Army. Both the North and South used balloons to scout the enemy's movements. Steiner took Zeppelin several hundred feet in the air. The balloon was tethered so it wouldn't fly off.

By then, aeronauts realized that to be truly useful, balloons needed to be steered and have a source of power so they could move horizontally and fly into the wind. In 1852 another Frenchman, Jules Henri Giffard, created a balloon that had a steam engine for power. On the world's first flight of a powered balloon, Giffard reached a speed of 6 miles (9.5 km) per hour. Two decades after the Civil War, French army officers built a balloon that used a battery-powered electric motor to travel and then return against the wind to its launching site. But the tests did not pave the way to long-distance air travel. Zeppelin and his dirigible held the key to that.

In 1890 Zeppelin retired from the army and began to pursue his dream of building a rigid airship. Helping the development process was the recent improvement of the internal combustion engine. Powered by gasoline or diesel fuel, this kind of engine would change transportation around the world. Gas engines were used to power some of the first cars and were soon put in boats. Some inventors put gas engines on small dirigibles. Meanwhile, Zeppelin spent several years raising money to build the first rigid airship.

Finally, in 1898, he began building the Luftschiff (Airship) *Zeppelin 1* inside a floating hangar on Germany's Bodensee. The lake borders Switzerland and is also called Lake Constance. Zeppelin thought it would be easier to land the craft on the lake than on the ground. And the hangar could be turned into the wind, regardless of its direction. By 1900 the *LZ-1* was ready for its test flight. The 420-foot-long (128 m) airship had 17 gas cells filled with hydrogen. Two gondolas, not far from the ends of the airship, had one engine apiece. The airship, however, was not completely steerable, and its engines were not big enough for a craft of that size. Soon Zeppelin was redesigning his dirigible.

Over the next eight years, Zeppelin and his engineers installed larger engines and added fins to help steer the aircraft. In 1908 *LZ-4* flew for 12 consecutive hours, carrying 12 people to Switzerland and back. The longest airplane flights of the time lasted only an hour or two.

Later that year Zeppelin created a company to build more dirigibles, and in 1909 it set up a separate company to develop passenger service using the airships. Starting in 1910, the German Airship Transportation Corporation carried the first of thousands of passengers on trips across Germany. It was the world's first airline.

With the outbreak of World War I in July 1914, Germany quickly put Zeppelin's rigid airships to

A 1908 zeppelin, most likely *LZ-4*, was launched from a floating hangar on the Bodensee in Germany.

military use. In late August a German zeppelin made history as the first aircraft to conduct a bombing raid on a city, attacking Antwerp, Belgium. The next year, Germany carried out more extensive bombing raids over England. The raids forced England to keep thousands of soldiers at home to fire the guns used to attack incoming zeppelins. Without the threat of the airships, the soldiers could have gone to France, the scene of some of the war's fiercest fighting. By 1916 the British had better defenses against the airships—

A British fighter plane successfully attacked a zeppelin in 1916.

high-flying fighter planes and incendiary bullets. Germany responded by creating new zeppelins that could reach much higher altitudes than England's planes. But height wasn't a guarantee of success. Many zeppelins were shot down as they descended to land.

The zeppelin did not play a major role in the last years of the war. And England and France, later joined by the United States, united to defeat Germany and its allies. The peace treaty Germany signed in 1919 forced it to give up some of its land and greatly reduced the size of its military. The country also had to pay reparations to the winning nations for the property it had destroyed.

Ferdinand von Zeppelin had died during the war. Hugo Eckener then ran the Zeppelin Company. Trained as a psychologist, Eckener had joined the company in 1909. Within two years he had learned how to fly dirigibles. An accident on his first flight had made him sensitive to the safety of flying airships. He once said, "It is absolutely necessary to know an operation will be successful before proceeding."

The peace treaty of 1919 limited the size of airships Germany could build, so to keep the Zeppelin Company alive, Eckener agreed to build one for the U.S. Navy. The *LZ-126* would serve as part of German reparations. Although meant for the U.S. Navy to use as a training aircraft, the *LZ-126* was also designed to carry passengers. It was the first airship to have beds. Completed in 1924, the new airship, later named the U.S.S. *Los Angeles,* was the largest zeppelin ever built until then. It could reach speeds of almost 80 miles (129 km) per hour.

To deliver the airship to the U.S., Eckener made the first flight of a German zeppelin over the Atlantic Ocean. When he reached New York, Eckener used a tiny parachute to send a message to the people below. It said, in part, "We will work hand in hand at the task of bridging time and distance, thereby binding all nations of the Earth more closely together."

Eckener was hailed as an aviation hero in Germany and the United States. The rigid airship was faster than a steamship, and no plane could carry as much as a zeppelin could. A treaty signed in Europe in 1925 ended the restrictions on German

The USS *Los Angeles* was mainly used as a training ship by the Navy.

The *Graf Zeppelin* flew over the U.S. Capitol in Washington, D.C.

airship production, and Eckener soon began to design the most advanced dirigible ever built. Completed in 1928, *LZ-127*, also called the *Graf Zeppelin*, was almost 800 feet (244 m) long and could carry enough fuel to travel more than 8,000 miles (12,875 km) without stopping.

Soon after its launch, the *Graf Zeppelin* made history when it completed the first transatlantic flight carrying paying customers. Eckener commanded the airship on the flight, and among the passengers was Charles Rosendahl, the future commander of the Lakehurst Naval Station. In 1929 the airship circled the globe, covering more than 21,000 miles (33,800 km) in five segments. It set a record for the fastest flight around the world, and thousands of people waited to greet the *Graf Zeppelin* when it completed its trip at Lakehurst. Soon after that achievement, Eckener made plans for regular passenger flights between Germany and Brazil.

But not everything was going smoothly for the world's airships. The British had just completed two dirigibles, and in 1930, one called *R-101* had crashed on its maiden flight to India. Almost all of the passengers had died in the fire that erupted when the airship's hydrogen ignited. The British soon pulled their other airship out of service. Even before this accident, Eckener had thought of a way to improve airship safety—using helium instead of hydrogen for lift. Unlike hydrogen, helium does not burn. When Eckener designed the *LZ-129*, soon to be called the *Hindenburg*, he hoped it would use helium. Because helium does not provide as much lift as hydrogen, the new airship had to be even bigger than the *Graf Zeppelin* to carry all the helium it needed.

There was a problem, though. The United States controlled the production of helium. It came from natural gas taken from the ground in several states. A 1927 law did not allow the gas to be sold overseas. So, although the *Hindenburg* could have been the safest passenger airship ever built, when it first flew it carried highly flammable hydrogen.

But not everything was going smoothly for the world's airships.

MORE DIRIGIBLE ACCIDENTS

The Akron, *which was designed for long-range scouting, was built in Akron, Ohio.*

While the Zeppelin Company worked on getting the *Hindenburg* airborne, two American dirigibles came to disastrous ends. Congress approved plans in 1926 to build two helium-filled airships for the Navy. Each of them would be an airborne aircraft carrier, carrying several small airplanes to be used for reconnaissance. The builder would be a joint company started several years before by the Goodyear Tire and Rubber Company and the Zeppelin Company.

The first of the two dirigibles, the *Akron,* was launched in 1931. Two years later the airship hit severe winds off the New Jersey coast and crashed into the ocean. All but three of the 76 people on board were killed, making it the deadliest airship accident ever. Errors made by the captain, Frank McCord, may have contributed to the crash.

The *Akron*'s sister ship, the *Macon*, was launched in 1933. It was based in California. In 1935 the *Macon* ran into a strong storm over the Pacific Ocean and crashed into the water. The Navy had not completely repaired earlier damage to one of its tail fins, which played a role in the accident. Two of its 76 crew members were killed. The *Macon* was the last rigid airship flown by the Navy.

Because of Eckener's and his company's experience, designing the *Hindenburg* was not hard. Getting it built and into the skies, however, was another story. The Great Depression hit the world in 1929, and when construction started on *LZ-129* in 1931, Eckener had trouble getting the money he needed. A boost came several years later, after the Nazi Party came to power in Germany. Led by Adolf Hitler, the Nazis thought the peace treaty that ended World War I had placed too much blame on Germany for that war. Hitler wanted to build a strong German military and unite all German-speaking Europeans under his rule.

In 1934 Nazi officials agreed to provide money to finish building the *Hindenburg*. Hitler believed Germans were part of a "master race" that stood above all other peoples on Earth. He and the Nazis blamed Germany's Jews for many of the country's ills. Soon after taking power in 1933, the Nazis passed laws to limit the legal rights of Jews. Completing and flying the largest airship of all time would be good propaganda. The *Hindenburg* would show the world the greatness of German technology. The airship would fly with swastikas painted on its tail. The swastika was the symbol of the Nazi Party.

The *Hindenburg* flew for the first time in March 1936. Within two months it began the first regular passenger service by air between Germany and the United States. The takeoff on the first flight was so

The *Hindenburg* was built in Friedrichshafen, Germany, on the shores of the Bodensee.

smooth that some passengers didn't even realize they were airborne. An American reporter on the flight wrote, "You feel as though you are carried in the arms of angels." The airship was so popular that the Zeppelin Company added more passenger cabins before the next flying season. The first North American flight of 1937 left Germany on May 3. It would be the *Hindenburg*'s last.

ChapterThree
DISASTER AT LAKEHURST

As the *Hindenburg* approached the mooring mast at Lakehurst on the evening of May 6, 1937, a group of passengers gathered one last time in the lounge by the promenade windows. The mood was cheerful, as people exchanged addresses and eagerly waited to see loved ones on the ground. Joseph Späh, a stage comic and acrobat, took pictures of the ground crew catching the first mooring line tossed from the airship. A crew member dropped a second line down. Then Späh saw a flash of light, followed by an explosion. The crew member assured the passengers everything was all right, but the stern of the *Hindenburg* plunged downward, and he and the other passengers fell to the deck. "We were a mass of shrieking, crying people," Späh said later. A second explosion soon followed. Earlier in the flight, Späh had chatted with Ernst Lehmann, a former captain of the airship. Späh had told Lehmann that he was a "flying jinx" because he had been in three air crashes. Lehmann told him, "You don't need to worry, my friend. Zeppelins never have accidents." That was about to change.

In another part of the *Hindenburg*, Leonhard Adelt stood at an open window and searched the ground for family members there to greet him. He saw some

News photographers were expecting a routine landing when disaster struck the *Hindenburg* at Lakehurst.

people in the crowd react strangely as the airship neared the mooring mast. He had heard a sound but hadn't thought anything of it. Now Adelt looked toward the stern and saw a red glow. He realized the *Hindenburg* was on fire.

As the ground crew and onlookers saw the first flames and heard the dull explosions, panic set in. Ground crewmen who were closest to the burning airship began to run from the landing site. Some relatives of the passengers started to scream. Others prayed for their loved ones' safety. Meanwhile, the news photographers and movie crews there to cover the landing recorded the unfolding disaster.

One of the photographers in the group was Sam Shere. He worked for International News Photos. The son of Russian immigrants, he had had an early interest in photography and movie making. As a boy, he had hung around Pathe Studios in New Jersey. The studio made some of the first movies ever produced, and Shere earned money for his family by carrying equipment for the photographers who worked there. He eventually learned about photography after moving to California and getting a job with a film studio there. The studios needed pictures of their stars for advertisements.

When he became a professional photographer, Shere liked to report on "hard news," events with political or social importance. In 1927 he photographed Charles Lindbergh as he began his famous solo airplane flight across the Atlantic Ocean. Shere was in northern France in 1930 and photographed the aftermath of the crash of the British dirigible *R-101*. Five years later he covered a court appearance by Bruno Hauptmann, who had been charged with kidnapping and murdering Lindbergh's baby. Shere surprised many of the other professional photographers when he pulled a small 35-millimeter camera out of his pocket. Most pros of the day used the much larger Speed Graphic camera. They considered the smaller camera a toy. The 35mm camera, however, was easier to use, and Shere

The *Hindenburg* floated toward the mooring mast seconds before it burst into flames.

thought its pictures were just as good as the ones taken with the Speed Graphic.

But on the day Shere went to Lakehurst for the *Hindenburg* landing, he carried his own Speed Graphic. He didn't think the airship's routine arrival was particularly newsworthy, especially since none of its passengers was very famous. The only important person, he thought, was Rolf von Heidenstamm, a Swedish businessman who also served in his country's government. Shere was there mostly to pick up photos being sent from Europe to U.S. news agencies.

When the first flames erupted, Shere was about 150 feet (46 m) from the mooring mast and did not have his camera at the ready. "I didn't even have time to get it up to my eye," he later said. "I literally 'shot' from the hip—it was over so fast there was nothing else to do." As he felt the heat from the fire on his skin, Shere took several pictures. The most famous one shows a gigantic ball of flames shooting skyward from the *Hindenburg* as its stern points toward the ground. Under the fireball, bits of flaming debris are falling like streams of light from exploding fireworks. The photo captured the disaster as it was still unfolding, before the entire airship crashed to the ground.

To some photography historians, one of the striking things about Shere's photo is its composition, given how quickly he took the picture. The airship seems divided in two. The fire consumes the rear half while the front looks as perfect as it did when it was first launched. The airship and the right leg of the mooring mast create a diagonal line across the picture. A vertical line is formed by the explosion and the mast itself. Areas of light and dark are spread throughout the image.

As university professors Robert Hariman and John Louis Lucaites wrote 70 years later, Shere's

Shere's famous photo captured the *Hindenburg* in the midst of disaster.

work is a "beautifully balanced representation of an unplanned, uncontrolled explosion."

As powerful as the image was, it could not capture all the panic and destruction caused by the fire. Shere pulled out his 35mm camera and photographed survivors escaping the flaming wreck. The pictures were so gruesome that he was only able to sell one of them.

Among the survivors was Philip Mangone, a New York business owner. While the *Hindenburg* was still airborne, he threw a chair through a window and climbed out onto a ledge. He jumped to the ground and then watched pieces of the burning wreckage fall around him. Joseph Späh also knocked out a window and then held onto a window ledge until the airship got close enough to the ground to safely let go. He fell about 40 feet (12 m). He hurt his ankle but managed to crawl away before flaming pieces of the *Hindenburg* could hit him. A sailor found him crawling on the ground in a daze. "A lot of us are alive," Spah managed to say.

He and Mangone survived, but others who jumped from the airship did not. Another victim was Ulla, a dog Späh was bringing home to his children. Many of the surviving passengers were badly burned. In some cases their clothes and hair had burned off their bodies. Sailors and civilians rushed over to guide the survivors to safety.

Perhaps the luckiest survivor was 14-year-old Werner Franz, who worked on the airship as a cabin boy. He was in the officers' dining room when he heard a noise and then felt the airship's stern plunge downward. Flames soon filled the room, and then a water tank burst. The water put out the flames around Werner and snapped him back to attention. He kicked out a hatch that was used to load supplies

AN AMATEUR'S PICTURES

Arthur Cofod Jr.'s hands shook as he photographed the Hindenburg *bursting into flames.*

Sam Shere and the other professional photographers at Lakehurst didn't take all the pictures of the *Hindenburg* disaster. Also there on the evening of May 6 was Arthur Cofod Jr. He owned a company that received and delivered packages for businesses. *Life* magazine had hired him to pick up photos being shipped to the magazine from Germany.

Cofod happened to bring his 35mm camera with him to Lakehurst, and he took a series of images of the *Hindenburg* that later appeared in *Life*. The first shows the airship's nose pointing down as it prepared to land.

The next came right after flames erupted from the zeppelin's stern. The picture is a little blurred, because Cofod's hands shook as he realized what was happening. The last shot of the sequence shows a thick black cloud filling the sky and covering most of the *Hindenburg* wreckage on the ground.

Since Cofod was not with the professional photographers, his shots were taken from an angle that was different from that of Shere's. Cofod's images also showed an advantage of a 35mm camera over the bigger Speed Graphic—it could take many pictures quickly.

Flames consumed the *Hindenburg* as it hit the ground.

on the *Hindenburg*. When the burning airship neared the ground, Werner jumped to safety.

In the *Hindenburg*'s control car, Captain Pruss and others waited until the forward section of the airship got lower to the ground before jumping. Seven got out before the nose of the ship bounced off the ground and back into the air. When it had dropped again, to about 15 feet (4.5 m) above the surface, Pruss and the others jumped. Pruss had been burned, but he ran back toward the wreckage to look for passengers. After two trips into the flames, three

Thick smoke rose from the still-burning *Hindenburg* after it crashed to the ground in flames.

sailors dragged Pruss to an ambulance. Other injured crewmen and passengers waited for ambulances as the odor of burning flesh drifted through the night air.

It had taken less than a minute for the *Hindenburg* to burn and crash, the fire ripping through its gas cells. Hot and blackened girders from the airship's metal frame were all that remained. Doctors and nurses from nearby towns rushed to the naval station to treat the wounded as best they could.

Shere and other photographers had given their

film to Pat O'Malley, who worked for American Airlines. The airline offered connecting flights for *Hindenburg* passengers to cities across the United States. O'Malley knew the photographers couldn't leave the scene, so she took the film on a plane to Newark, New Jersey. Waiting for her were motorcycle messengers, who took the film to the news outlets that had sent photographers to Lakehurst.

The next day millions of Americans saw Shere's picture of the *Hindenburg* or one of the similar photos that other photographers had taken. International News Photo sold its pictures to many newspapers, and Shere's photo ended up on the front page of the *Washington Post*. It also appeared in *Life*, a magazine famous for its news photos. Shere's shot was named the best news picture of 1937 by *Editor & Publisher*, a magazine that covers the journalism business. Years later, photography historian Beaumont Newhall used Shere's shot to illustrate some of the best photojournalism of the 20th century in a book on the history of photography.

The impact of Shere's photo strengthened the idea among newspaper publishers that they needed to have photographers on the scene of important events. Of course, the trick was knowing ahead of time what events would be important. No one suspected the *Hindenburg* would so spectacularly crash that day.

Many people also saw the newsreel footage of the accident. Some people were said to have fainted in

Sam Shere posed in front of the wreckage the day after the *Hindenburg* disaster. He held his Speed Graphic camera and wore his 35mm Leica around his neck.

movie theaters when they saw badly burned victims or people falling from the flaming dirigible to their deaths. Some viewers screamed in horror, shocked by seeing the disaster on the big screen. Scenes of violence were less common then than they are today. Images of brutal death were not allowed in Hollywood films then, and no one had television sets

in their homes to show them gruesome news events. Years later some films combined the moving image with radio reporter Herbert Morrison's account of the disaster as it happened.

By midnight, the scene at Lakehurst had calmed somewhat. Survivors who needed medical attention were in nearby hospitals. The bodies of the dead lay in the station's hangar, which normally housed dirigibles. A guard stood watch over what was left of the *Hindenburg*, to make sure no one disturbed it.

The final death count from the disaster was 36. All but one were among the 97 passengers and crew who had made the flight from Germany. The other victim was a member of the ground crew. Of the *Hindenburg's* dead, 13 were passengers and 22 were crew members. The dead included Ernst Lehmann, a former captain of the *Hindenburg*.

On May 7, as news of the *Hindenburg* disaster spread around the world, workers began examining the wreckage. Little of the luggage on board survived the fire, and just 358 of the more than 17,000 pieces of mail were recovered. The workers also found a German pistol. When some newspaper reporters learned of this, they wondered whether a German crew member had killed himself rather than die in the fiery crash. But no one ever proved that that's what had happened.

In Germany and elsewhere, people who had been convinced of the *Hindenburg's* safety could not believe the news. One of them was Hugo Eckener of the Zeppelin Company. A reporter called Eckener in the middle of the night and told him what had happened at Lakehurst. "No, it isn't possible," the dirigible expert said. A call from someone in the German government in the morning confirmed the news. Eckener later wrote his wife, "I deeply regret that I was persuaded to allow the use of hydrogen when the *Hindenburg*, after all, had been designed for the use of helium."

ChapterFour
END OF AN ERA

For officials in both Germany and the United States, the most pressing question on May 7 and during the following weeks was: What caused the fiery end of the *Hindenburg*? Even before the airship left Germany, the German Embassy in Washington, D.C., had received a letter warning the Zeppelin Company to check all the mail carried on the airship. It said, "The Zeppelin is going to be destroyed by a time bomb during its flight to another country." This letter was not the first of its kind, and usually such letters were simply ignored. But after May 6, Eckener and other Germans wondered whether some sort of sabotage had brought down the *Hindenburg*. The Nazi Party had enemies both inside and outside Germany. Destroying the airship would have been a blow to German pride and Adolf Hitler's attempt to portray the greatness of Germany under his rule.

Germany's leaders wanted to end any thought of sabotage directed against the Nazis. They ordered Eckener to give speeches in both German and English to stress that sabotage was not likely. Eckener left for New Jersey to help figure out what had caused the disaster. He led a German team of investigators, and the Americans had their own team. Both teams reached the same conclusion: There was no evidence that sabotage had destroyed the *Hindenburg*.

> But after May 6, Eckener and other Germans wondered whether some sort of sabotage had brought down the *Hindenburg*.

Reporters surrounded Hugo Eckener after he arrived in New Jersey to lead an investigation into the crash.

So what had? The most reasonable explanation was that a leak in a gas cell let hydrogen escape into the air. Then something had ignited the mixture of hydrogen and air, causing a fire that spread quickly. Witnesses who appeared before the U.S. commission investigating the disaster offered several theories. The possible causes that were rejected included sparks from the engines' exhaust and a short circuit in the airship's electrical system.

American investigators studied the scene a few days after the crash.

Both the German and American investigative reports agreed that the *Hindenburg*'s hydrogen had likely been ignited by a static discharge. It was most probably from a buildup of static electricity caused by the thunderstorm conditions at the landing field. The ignition also might have been caused by St. Elmo's fire, the name for an electrical charge sometimes seen around masts of ships when they sail through thunderstorms.

But some people refused to give up the idea of sabotage. Years later Captain Max Pruss still believed someone had planted a bomb aboard or in some other way caused the fire and explosion. Rosendahl, commander of Lakehurst and a friend of Eckener's, had heard the German's private theory that sabotage brought down the *Hindenburg*. Less than two weeks after the disaster, Rosendahl met with representatives of the FBI, and the agency reported that he "is confident that there was sabotage present in connection with the destruction" of the *Hindenburg*.

The same FBI report noted that crew members had seen Joseph Späh alone in parts of the ship where passengers were not allowed without a crew member with them. Späh roamed freely as he went to take care of his dog, Ulla, and another dog making the trip. The dogs were kept in a storage room near where the fire started. Crew members also claimed that Späh had spoken out against the Nazi Party. The FBI investigated Späh and concluded he had nothing to do with the disaster.

Years later two writers suggested that a crew member named Eric Spehl could have carried out sabotage. His job gave him access to the gas cells, and he was known to oppose the Nazi Party. But once again, no one had proof that Spehl or anyone else had carried out sabotage.

The *Hindenburg* disaster and the photos of it, like Shere's, changed the world's perceptions of airships that flew with hydrogen. Though the *Graf Zeppelin* had gone years without an accident, it immediately

stopped flying. Any future airships would have to use helium. The idea of the "indestructible" airship made some people remember the *Titanic*. That supposedly unsinkable ocean liner struck an iceberg and sank on its first voyage in 1912. To some, the accident in Lakehurst made the *Hindenburg* "the *Titanic* of the skies." Both disasters showed that even the greatest technological marvels face risks.

Germany was already building a sister ship to the *Hindenburg*, which came to be called *LZ-130 Graf Zeppelin*. Eckener persuaded President Franklin Roosevelt to ease the restriction on selling helium to foreign countries. He argued, in part, that modern warplanes had made it impractical to use the dirigibles militarily. Helium, he said, would only be used for passenger flights.

With the promise of American helium, the Zeppelin Company began to modify the new airship so it could fly with the safe gas. But German aggression soon ended the new agreement with the Americans. As part of his plan to take over large parts of Europe, Hitler sent German troops into Austria in March 1938. The threat of a larger European war rose because of Germany's actions. Soon Harold Ickes, U.S. secretary of the interior, ordered that the supply of helium be shut off again. When asked why, Ickes told Eckener, "Because your Hitler is preparing for war. ... With a helium-filled ship you could fly over London and drop bombs." A newspaper in St. Louis, Missouri, agreed with the decision, saying: "Dr. Eckener, we like you and your Zeppelin, and would be glad to give you helium, but you will understand that we cannot give helium to a liar, thief and murderer like Hitler."

When the new *Graf Zeppelin* flew for the first time later in 1938, it carried hydrogen in its cells. But it never carried paying passengers. Between its launch and the start of World War II in September 1939, the Germans used it only for propaganda purposes and reconnaissance. Once the war began, the Nazis turned both airships named *Graf Zeppelin* into scrap and demolished the zeppelin hangar at the Frankfurt airport. Even before the *Hindenburg* disaster, aviation experts could see that airplanes, not airships, would come to dominate long-distance travel. Improved technology made planes much faster and less expensive to operate. Only the wealthy would be able to afford the time and cost of traveling by dirigible. But the destruction of the *Hindenburg* stopped passenger airship travel sooner than it might have ended. And it had followed the disasters of the *Macon*, *Akron*, and *R-101*. Some people had a growing sense that carrying passengers on airships might not be worth the risk.

But while rigid airships like the zeppelins largely stopped flying, blimps still sail the skies. The U.S. Navy used helium-filled blimps during World War II to patrol the coasts of the United States, searching for enemy submarines. The Navy flew blimps until 1962, and then started again in 2010, using them for reconnaisance and to carry out scientific experiments. Businesses use them for advertising, putting their names on the blimps and flying them over sporting events.

Photos like Sam Shere's were the first to capture an air disaster as it happened. That's one reason people are still fascinated by the *Hindenburg*. Others are impressed by the engineering skills that created such a large and beautiful airship. It remains the largest aircraft ever to fly. And some people still

A Navy blimp was readied for patrol duty along the East Coast in 1943 during World War II.

try to prove or disprove what caused the fire that destroyed the airship. Many new theories have emerged since 1937, but none has settled the issue.

A scientist named Addison Bain suggested in 1997 that the hydrogen in the airship was not the source of the fire. Instead, he said, it was the covering over the gas cells. The fabric was painted with a substance called dope that contained various chemicals. Some of those substances, Bain said, were highly flammable under the right conditions—such as when an electrical charge was present. Since the early 2000s, several scientists, along with the TV show *Mythbusters*, have shown that the covering was not highly flammable and therefore was not the source of the fire. In 2013 a documentary shown on American and British TV confirmed the original static electricity theory, with the charge coming from the airship itself.

For Shere, his famous photo was just one episode in a long career. In the years afterward, he spent some time traveling with and photographing Winston Churchill, Great Britain's leader during World War II.

A blimp appeared to greet an ocean liner sailing into New York harbor in a 1946 photograph by Sam Shere.

RETURN OF THE AIRSHIP

The Hybrid Airship *can carry people and cargo to remote locations.*

Blimps still fly in the skies, and a German company named for Ferdinand von Zeppelin still makes airships. The new models are called semi-rigid—they have some metal framing to support the load the airship carries. The *Zeppelin NT* was introduced in 1997 to carry passengers. Since then, the Goodyear Tire and Rubber Company has replaced its well-known blimps with the new helium-filled zeppelins.

In the United States, Lockheed Martin has introduced a nonrigid airship called the *Hybrid Airship*. Also filled with helium, like all the modern airships, it can carry up to 23 tons (21 metric tons) of cargo to remote areas. The *Hybrid Airship* can reach speeds of 70 miles (113 km) per hour and carry up to 19 passengers along with its cargo. A British company is also testing a new nonrigid airship called the *Airlander 10*. Hybrid Air

Vehicles, maker of the new airship, says it will be able to fly missions for up to three weeks without a crew onboard, making it ideal for reconnaissance. The airship is housed in the same hangar that was once home to the *R-101*, the British airship that crashed in France in 1930. Hybrid Air has plans to make an even larger version of the 300-foot (91-m) long *Airlander 10*.

The rigid airship is also returning to the skies, thanks to a U.S. company called Worldwide Aeros. It has designed an airship called the *Aeroscraft*. The airship is the size of a football field and, like the Lockheed Martin aircraft, can carry heavy loads of cargo to areas that lack railways and airports. Its engines tilt, so the airship can take off and land like a helicopter. Worldwide Aeros also makes the *Sky Dragon*, a smaller airship designed for patrolling borders or gathering intelligence.

He also photographed other world leaders, including several presidents and Queen Elizabeth II. During World War II, Shere covered battles and took pictures from U.S. military planes as they carried out their missions. Looking back over his career, Shere said he had a knack for being cool under pressure. He also said, "I seemed always to be at the right place at the right time."

Along with the famous photos, the story of the *Hindenburg* has been kept alive with books and movies and various uses of Shere's photo. When the rock band Led Zeppelin released its first album in 1969, the cover featured a stylized version of Shere's shot. Shere's image has also appeared on posters and in art. The film footage shot as the disaster happened is widely available on the Internet. Most videos include Herbert Morrison's radio coverage.

His phrase "Oh, the humanity!" is still well known today. In 2015 the airline JetBlue used its own version of the phrase on Twitter. Some people thought "Oh, the Bluemanity!" was in poor taste, since it referred to an air disaster that cost 36 lives. JetBlue quickly removed the tweet and apologized for it.

The *Hindenburg* disaster helped spell the end of commercial airships. But Sam Shere's picture captured a moment of horror that continues to fascinate people around the world.

Led Zeppelin's 1969 studio album featured the burning *Hindenburg*.

Timeline

1898

Count Ferdinand von Zeppelin begins building his first rigid airship

1900

The *LZ-1* flies for the first time

1924

Hugo Eckener makes the first transatlantic crossing in a zeppelin with the USS *Los Angeles*

1927

The United States prohibits the sale of helium to foreign countries, forcing Germany's zeppelins to use flammable hydrogen instead

1910

The German Airship Transportation Corporation begins carrying passengers on its zeppelins

1914

Germany uses a zeppelin to carry out the world's first air bombing raid; zeppelins would continue to be used in World War I

1928

The *Graf Zeppelin* makes the first transatlantic zeppelin flight with paying passengers

1930

The British dirigible *R-101* crashes and burns in France

Timeline

1933

The U.S. Navy airship *Akron* crashes off the coast of New Jersey, killing 73 people

1935

The U.S. Navy airship *Macon* crashes off the coast of California, killing two people

1937

On May 6, the *Hindenburg* catches fire while landing at Lakehurst; Sam Shere's photo of the disaster is named the best news photograph of the year

1997

German company introduces a semi-rigid airship, the *Zeppelin NT*

1936

The *Hindenburg* makes its first flight to Lakehurst, New Jersey

2013

California company begins flight testing the *Aeroscraft* rigid airship

2016

British and American companies launch helium-filled airships, the world's biggest aircraft

Glossary

aeronauts—people who travel in balloons or other aircraft

alloy—material made by combining two or more metallic elements

control car—gondola on a zeppelin that contains the instruments for steering it

gondola—compartment suspended below an airship

hull—main body of a rigid airship

incendiary—designed to cause fires

knot—unit of speed at sea or in the air; 1 knot equals 1.15 miles per hour

photojournalism—use of photography to capture events and persons in the news

propaganda—information spread to try to influence the thinking of people; often not completely true or fair

reconnaissance—scouting an area to see what it looks like and whether it has any dangers

reparations—payments made to make amends for wrongdoing

sabotage—to damage, destroy, or disrupt on purpose

tethered—tied with a rope or chain to restrict movement

Additional Resources

Further Reading

Curley, Robert, ed. *The Complete History of Aviation: From Ballooning to Supersonic Flight.* New York: Britannica Educational Publishing, 2012.

Hawkins, John. *Air Disasters.* New York: Rosen Central, 2012.

Otfinoski. Steven. *The Hindenburg Explosion: Core Events of a Disaster in the Air.* North Mankato, Minn.: Capstone Press, 2014.

Internet Sites

Use FactHound to find Internet sites related to this book. All of the sites on FactHound have been researched by our staff.

Here's all you do:
Visit *www.facthound.com*
Type in this code: 9780756554415

Critical Thinking Using the Common Core

Why did Adolf Hitler agree to provide money to complete the building of the *Hindenburg*? (Key Ideas and Details)

Photographer Sam Shere used both a Speed Graphic and 35mm camera. What was one advantage of the smaller 35mm camera over the Speed Graphic? (Craft and Structure)

Why was the *Hindenburg* called "the *Titanic* of the skies" after it burned and crashed? (Key Ideas and Details)

Source Notes

Page 4, line 21: "Winds Delay Hindenburg; German Airship Expected Here This Evening, 12 Hours Late." *The New York Times.* 6 May 1937, p. 8.

Page 5, line 3: Ibid.

Page 11, line 14: "Commerce Department Accident Report on the Hindenburg Disaster." 15 Aug. 1937. 11 May 2016. Airships: A Hindenburg and Zeppelin History Site. http://www.airships.net/hindenburg/disaster/commerce-department-report

Page 12, line 9: Ibid.

Page 14, line 9: Herbert Morrison, WLS Radio (Chicago) Address on the Hindenburg Disaster, 6 May 1937. 11 May 2016. American Rhetoric Online Speech Bank. http://www.americanrhetoric.com/speeches/hindenburgcrash.htm

Page 14, line 14: Douglas Botting. *Dr. Eckener's Dream Machine: The Great Zeppelin and the Dawn of Air Travel.* New York: H. Holt, 2001, p. 276

Page 14, line 16: Ibid.

Page 14, line 21: Herbert Morrison, WLS Radio (Chicago) Address on the Hindenburg Disaster.

Page 18, line 2: Tim Sharp. "The First Hot-Air Balloon." Space.com. 16 July 2012. 11 May 2016. http://www.space.com/16595-montgolfiers-first-balloon-flight.html

Page 23, line 15: "Hugo Eckener." Airships: A Hindenburg and Zeppelin History Site. 11 May 2016. http://www.airships.net/hugo-eckener

Page 24, line 5: *Dr. Eckener's Dream Machine: The Great Zeppelin and the Dawn of Air Travel*, p. 102.

Page 29, line 3: Ibid., p. 266.

Page 30, line 14: United Press. "Survivor Describes Jump from Blazing Hindenburg." *The Pittsburgh Press.* 8 May 1937, p. 2. 13 May 2016. https://news.google.com/newspapers?nid=djft3U1LymYC&dat=19370508&printsec=frontpage&hl=en

Page 30, line 20: John Toland. *The Great Dirigibles: Their Triumphs and Disasters.* New York: Dover Publications, 1972, p. 312.

Page 34, line 5: "History as It Happened: The Photographs That Defined Our Times." *The Telegraph.* 11 May 2016. http://www.telegraph.co.uk/expat/expatpicturegalleries/8502342/History-as-it-happened-the-photographs-that-defined-our-times.html

Page 35, line 1: Robert Hariman and John Louis Lucaites. *No Caption Needed: Iconic Photographs, Public Culture, and Liberal Democracy.* Chicago: University of Chicago Press, 2007, p. 249.

Page 36, line 12: *The Great Dirigibles: Their Triumphs and Disasters*, p. 332

Page 43, line 23: Ibid., p. 336.

Page 43, line 27: *Dr. Eckener's Dream Machine: The Great Zeppelin and the Dawn of Air Travel*, p. 285.

Page 44, line 8: Ibid., p. 272.

Page 47, line 6: "FBI–Hindenburg." FBI Records: The Vault – Hindenburg. 11 May 2016. https://vault.fbi.gov/Hindenburg%20/Hindenburg%20Part%201%20of%204/view

Page 48, line 6: Kasia Cieplak-Mayr von Baldegg. "Recovered Letters Reveal the Lost History of the Hindenburg." *The Atlantic.* 19 April 2012. 13 May 2016. http://www.theatlantic.com/technology/archive/2012/04/recovered-letters-reveal-the-lost-history-of-the-hindenburg/467973/

Page 49, line 14: *Dr. Eckener's Dream Machine: The Great Zeppelin and the Dawn of Air Travel*, p. 292.

Page 49, line 18: Ibid., p. 291.

Page 54, line 7: Nanette Holland. "Spectating Brought Him Fame." *Gainesville Sun.* 7 May 1982, p. 1. 13 May 2016. https://news.google.com/newspapers?nid=dBzKUGQurMsC&dat=19820507&printsec=frontpage&hl=en

Page 54, line 20: Lily Rothman. "Why a JetBlue Tweet About 'Bluemanity' Was Controversial." *Time.* 26 Feb. 2015. 13 May 2016. http://time.com/3725101/jetblue-hindenburg-tweet/

Select Bibliography

Airships: A Hindenburg and Zeppelin History Site. http://www.airships.net

Botting, Douglas. *Dr. Eckener's Dream Machine: The Great Zeppelin and the Dawn of Air Travel*. New York: H. Holt, 2001.

Daily Mail reporter. "Hindenburg mystery solved 76 years after historic catastrophe: static electricity caused the airship to explode." *The Daily Mail*. 3 March 2013. 13 May 2016. http://www.dailymail.co.uk/news/article-2287608/Hindenburg-mystery-solved-76-years-historic-catastrophe-static-electricity-caused-airship-explode.html

Faber, John. *Great News Photos and the Stories Behind Them*. New York: Dover Publications, 1978

"FBI–Hindenburg." FBI Records: The Vault – Hindenburg. 11 May 2016. https://vault.fbi.gov/Hindenburg%20/Hindenburg%20Part%201%20of%204/view

Gambino, Megan. "Document Deep Dive: A Firsthand Account of the Hindenburg Disaster." Smithsonian.com. 1 May 2012. 13 May 2016. http://www.smithsonianmag.com/history/document-deep-dive-a-firsthand-account-of-the-hindenburg-disaster-79086828/?no-ist

Greatrex, Dana. "Photographer Sam Shere Vacations in New Smyrna." *Daytona Beach Morning Journal*, New Smyrna Edition. 19 Jan. 1978, p. 3. 13 May 2016. https://news.google.com/newspapers?nid=1873&dat=19780119&id=rlQgAAAAIBAJ&sjid=HdMEAAAAIBAJ&pg=1289,1012977&hl=en

Hariman, Robert, and John Louis Lucaites. *No Caption Needed: Iconic Photographs, Public Culture, and Liberal Democracy*. Chicago: University of Chicago Press, 2007.

Herbert Morrison, WLS Radio (Chicago) Address on the Hindenburg Disaster, 6 May 1937. 11 May 2016. American Rhetoric Online Speech Bank. http://www.americanrhetoric.com/speeches/hindenburgcrash.htm

Herbert Morrison audio. http://www.americanrhetoric.com/mp3clips/speeches/herbmorrisonhindenburgdisaster.mp3

Hindenburg Disaster Real Footage (1937). 13 May 2016. https://www.youtube.com/watch?v=CgWHbpMVQ1U

"History as It Happened: The Photographs That Defined Our Times." *The Telegraph*. 11 May 2016. http://www.telegraph.co.uk/expat/expatpicturegalleries/8502342/History-as-it-happened-the-photographs-that-defined-our-times.html

Holland, Nanette. "Spectating Brought Him Fame." *Gainesville Sun*. 7 May 1982, p. 1. 13 May 2016. https://news.google.com/newspapers?nid=dBzKUGGQurMsC&dat=19820507&printsec=frontpage&hl=en

Laskas, Jeanne Marie. "Helium Dreams: A new generation of airships is born." *The New Yorker*. 29 Feb. 2016. 13 May 2016. http://www.newyorker.com/magazine/2016/02/29/a-new-generation-of-airships-is-born

"Life on the American Newsfront: The Hindenburg Makes Her Last Landing at Lakehurst." *Life*. 17 May 1937. 13 May 2016. https://books.google.com/books?id=xkQEAAAAMBAJ&pg=PA26&dq=Hindenburg+life+magazine+1937&cd=6#v=onepage&q&f=false

Newhall, Beaumont. *The History of Photography: From 1839 to the Present*. Boston: Little, Brown, 1988.

Porter, Russell B. "Hindenburg Burns in Lakehurst Crash; 21 Known Dead, 12 Missing; 64 Escape." *The New York Times*. 7 May 1937, p. 1.

Rothman, Lily. "Why a JetBlue Tweet About 'Bluemanity' Was Controversial." *Time*. 26 Feb. 2015. 13 May 2016. http://time.com/3725101/jetblue-hindenburg-tweet/

Sharp, Tim. "The First Hot-Air Balloon." Space.com. 16 July 2012. 11 May 2016. http://www.space.com/16595-montgolfiers-first-balloon-flight.html

Special cable to The New York Times. "Planning Another Raid; Next One May Be Attempted on Kaiser's Birthday." *The New York Times*. 22 Jan. 1915, p. 2.

Toland, John. *The Great Dirigibles: Their Triumphs and Disasters*. New York: Dover Publications, 1972.

Toland, John. "Terror in the Twilight." *The Saturday Evening Post*. 8 Dec. 1956. http://www.saturdayeveningpost.com/wp-content/uploads/satevepost/hindenburg_explosion.pdf

Tucker, Abigail. "Found: Letters from the Hindenburg." *Smithsonian Magazine*. May 2012. 13 May 2016. http://www.smithsonianmag.com/arts-culture/found-letters-from-the-hindenburg-61380742/?no-ist=

United Press. "Survivor Describes Jump from Blazing Hindenburg." *The Pittsburgh Press*. 8 May 1937, p. 2. 13 May 2016. https://news.google.com/newspapers?nid=djft3U1LymYC&dat=19370508&printsec=frontpage&hl=en

Von Baldegg, Kasia Cieplak-Mayr. "Recovered Letters Reveal the Lost History of the Hindenburg." *The Atlantic*. 19 April 2012. 13 May 2016. http://www.theatlantic.com/technology/archive/2012/04/recovered-letters-reveal-the-lost-history-of-the-hindenburg/467973/

Wasel, Charla. "His Photographs Mirrored a Busy Life." *The Evening Independent*, St. Petersburg, Fla. 5 Oct. 1978, p. 1-B. 13 May 2016. https://news.google.com/newspapers?nid=PZE8UkGerEcC&dat=19781005&printsec=frontpage&hl=en

Weber, Bruce. "Werner Franz, Survivor of the Hindenburg's Crew, Dies at 92." *The New York Times*. 29 Aug. 2014. 13 May 2016. http://www.nytimes.com/2014/08/31/world/europe/werner-franz-survivor-of-the-hindenburgs-crew-dies-at-92.html

"Winds Delay Hindenburg; German Airship Expected Here This Evening, 12 Hours Late." *The New York Times*. 6 May 1937, p. 8.

Index

About the Adviser

Aviation historian Dan Grossman has been researching the technology and history of rigid airships and zeppelins for more than 20 years. His educational website, www.airships.net offers a wealth of information. Grossman lives in Atlanta, Georgia.

About the Author

Michael Burgan has written many books for children and young adults during his 20 years as a freelance writer. Most of his books have focused on history. Burgan has won several awards for his writing. He lives in Santa Fe, New Mexico.